ABOUT THE A

Both Lyn Fleet and Helen Roberts are m
Dog Trainers (APDT Member No.s
organisation was founded by the late Johr
nationwide network of trainers who woul kind, fair, and effective methods.

Both Lyn and Helen have a particular interest in, and understanding of, puppy development. This is a short, but crucial, time in a dog's life. Many behaviour problems that arise later on in a dog's life could have been prevented by a careful, structured, and 'busy' upbringing.

The information contained in this booklet comes from years of experience living with their own dogs, and helping clients cope with that happy but fraught time that is their dog's childhood. They hope that, by reading this booklet and putting the advice into practise, they can help you give your puppy the best possible start in life.

The K9 Kindergarten run by Lyn and Helen is always over-subscribed and has become a by-word with many local vets for best practise.

Please note:

Within this booklet, the dog is always referred to as 'he' for ease of reading. The advice given applies to both sexes.

(Illustrations by Dave Wilde, Mobility Instructor, Guide Dogs for the Blind Association

ISBN Number 0-9546845-0-8

This book is published by Lyn Fleet & Helen Roberts

CONTENTS

SETTLING YOUR PUPPY INTO HIS NEW HOME

The first few days in a new home are very stressful for a puppy. Suddenly, he's away from his family and no longer has his brothers and sisters for company and to play with. From now on, you are his mum and his siblings! He will look to you for nourishment and comfort, as well as fun and playtime.

The first night will be particularly worrying. Your puppy may howl, bark, whine, scratch at the door (or 'all of the above', if you're really unlucky). You can deal with this in different ways:

Sleep downstairs with your puppy. This means your puppy will automatically come to you for comfort and security (which helps the bonding process enormously) and you can hear when he needs to go to the toilet (which helps with house-training). Should this be impractical (or if your lumbago rules out this option), the second option would be the next best thing.

Take your puppy upstairs with you to the bedroom. Place him in a large cardboard box or an indoor kennel if you have been wise enough to buy one (see our section on Indoor Kennels) with a blanket for comfort. Once again, he can sense your closeness and this will comfort him. And again, if he needs to go to the toilet in the middle of the night you will hear him and be able to rush him outside.

Once your puppy has settled in, the bed can be moved gradually downstairs. Move the box or indoor kennel out onto the landing, then down into the hall, and then to wherever you have decided its final place should be. If you have invested in an indoor kennel, he will quickly realise that his bed is wherever his indoor kennel is.

The best place for your puppy's bed on a permanent basis is in a room with a washable floor, and away from the soft furnishings. Many people choose the kitchen or utility room. Make sure your pup has comfortable bedding in a draught-free area. Don't bother buying an expensive bed just yet as it will get chewed. Instead, invest in some sturdy cardboard boxes that can be easily replaced when they are treated to some special attention from your pup's jaws!

Some people still believe in the out-dated method of leaving the puppy downstairs and accept that no-one's going to get much sleep for a while. They believe the puppy should be left to cry as they know that, sooner or later, it will stop crying for the help and comfort that never arrives. While this may work, it does nothing for the bonding process or your puppy's emotional well-being.

Recognise that this is an unsettling time for your puppy. Give him time to adjust.

SIMPLE HOUSE RULES

Like us, dogs are social creatures living in a family unit (or pack). In these units there will be someone who makes decisions and there will be clearly defined roles. Your puppy will instinctively search for people he can rely on. He will thrive on consistency, routine and clear boundaries. The way you and your family behave will have the greatest impact on how your puppy relates to you.

Listed below are the main areas where your puppy will become confused and get himself into trouble if he isn't given those clear guidelines on how you would like him to behave.

Eating: A puppy begging for food is crushingly cute and almost impossible to resist! However, the full-grown dog who has learned to constantly pester, paw at you, slobber, whine and bark, is unlikely to impress the in-laws! It'll be the reason why your social life has taken a nose-dive and your friends and family are avoiding calling round. Preventing confusion is simple – don't give him little tasters while you're eating. If you'd like your puppy to share in your culinary masterpieces put some in his bowl for him to enjoy later.

Sleeping: Some puppies grow into dogs who take 'King of the Castle' to its ultimate level, defending the couch at all costs, while upstairs any attempt by you to sneak in under the duvet is met with swift rebuttal. Again, preventing confusion is simple – give him a comfortable, draught-free bed of his own. In this way, you'll both have peaceful nights (if only you could stop your partner snoring!!).

Playing: It's rude to interrupt. If you're reading the newspaper or watching the television, your pup should not be demanding that you play a game with him! Always start and end the games yourself. You decide when to play, for how long, and what the game will be. Remember that training, using reward-based methods, can also be seen as a game.

Attention: As with games, you decide when to give attention and for how long. Don't allow your pup to pester you for a fuss. When your pup is lying quietly, call him to you for a cuddle. Often, people ignore a quiet puppy because it's the first peace they've had for hours! But look at it from his point of view: when he's lying quietly, people ignore him, and that's no fun at all. If he learns that lying quietly means he gets praise and attention, he's more likely to choose that option.

N.B. As your puppy matures into a well-mannered adult, you can, if you wish, bend the rules slightly. Invite him for a cuddle on the sofa once in a while, but make sure he understands that it's a privilege that's not to be taken for granted. If you want him next to you, ask him to sit and wait before inviting him up. Only do this if you can be sure that he will get off again when you ask him.

FEEDING THE NEW ARRIVAL

A reputable breeder will have given you a feeding guide and a small supply of the diet your puppy is familiar with. Try not to change his feeding regime in the first week, as he has enough to cope with without new food upsetting his tummy (and it does nothing for all your hard work on the house-training front!).

If you are unsure, or if you have received no advice, ask your veterinary surgeon.

We recommend that, once adult, he stays on two meals per day for the rest of his life (unless instructed otherwise by your veterinary surgeon). Imagine what it would be like only having one meal per day! It would be so boring and by the 23rd hour the rumbling from your stomach would convince your neighbours that an earthquake was on the way!

Don't be tempted to spice up your puppy's diet by adding tasty morsels in order to tempt him to eat. This will make him a fussy eater which will play havoc with his digestive system as a young puppy needs particular vitamins and minerals in correct levels and proportions if he is to grow up to be healthy.

When your puppy was with his litter-mates, he had to push his way past his brothers and sisters for a fair portion of food. Now that the competition is gone, he may show less interest in his food. Accept what is happening and, if he decides to ignore his food, pick up the bowl after about ten minutes and save it for his next meal time.

NOTE: Fresh clean drinking water must be available for your puppy at all times. While your puppy is having accidents overnight, it can be tempting to restrict his access to water at certain times. However, this can be dangerous and detrimental to your puppy's health as he can dehydrate quickly. Dehydration can send a young animal's body into shock very quickly. Shock can kill.

HOW PUPPIES LEARN

Three quick, simple rules to get the best out of your puppy and get R.I.D. of behaviours you don't want:

REWARD behaviour you like. E.g. if you want your puppy to sit when meeting people, reward him for sitting by stroking him or giving him a treat.

IGNORE your dog when he's doing something you don't like. E.g. if he jumps up to say hello, turn your back on him and act as though you can't even see him.

DISTRACT your dog if he's going something you don't want but can't ignore. E.g., if he's going to jump up on Great Aunty Nelly who's just had a hip operation, distract him by throwing his toy in the opposite direction or giving him a stuffed Kong to chew.

What works and what doesn't work: Dogs repeat what they find most rewarding. Unfortunately, we don't always agree with them! Your puppy may, for instance, jump up to say hello (fine when he's a puppy, downright dangerous when he's fully grown – even a small dog could overbalance a frail, elderly person or a child). Or maybe he grabs the TV remote and races round the room with it. Why does he think this works? Because he gets lots of your attention for it. Your attention is a massive reward for your dog, which is why you must only give it on YOUR terms.

What can we use as a reward?
A reward is **anything** your puppy wants **at a particular time.** Think of all the things he enjoys. He may enjoy food, playing a game, a favourite toy, and having your undivided attention. For most puppies, your attention is the biggest reward you can give. Again, this is why it should not be available 'on demand' for your dog. If your attention is freely available, it loses its value.
We keep repeating this – can you tell how important we think it is?

They also learn **<u>what's safe and what's dangerous.</u>** If you are watching TV and you are suddenly aware that the pup is chewing the leg of the coffee table, your puppy will see you turn a different colour, the veins stand out on your neck, and you start leaping up and down, screaming hysterically! However, when you've calmed down and decide to make yourself a quick cuppa, your puppy is still left with the problem of how to ease his terribly uncomfortable gums. Having the memory span of a goldfish, he starts to chew the coffee table again. Nothing happens because you aren't there to see him. He learns that it's very dangerous to chew certain things while you're in the room, but it's safe to do it when you aren't there.

Don't make the common mistake of thinking your puppy has done this to defy you, or pay you back. Dogs don't think in terms of 'right and wrong'. He only thinks 'is it safe, or is it dangerous?'

If you chastise your puppy, you may see him looking sheepish. He slinks low to the floor, he looks up at you pathetically, he may even roll onto his back. ***<u>This is not guilt.</u>*** Remember, he doesn't think in terms of 'right and wrong', so he cannot feel guilt.

The 'sheepish' look is called 'submission'. In dog language, this is a way of relieving tension and deflecting aggression. Think how scared he must feel when he realises that it makes humans become even more aggressive! Not a good way to start a lifetime's relationship, is it?

HOUSETRAINING

Puppies have an in-built desire to keep their 'nest' clean. Your job is to persuade them that their 'nest' is the inside of your house. This can be an easy task if you understand how your puppy's toilet habits work.

Puppies are more likely to go to the toilet at specific times:

- When they've just woken from a long sleep or a nap
- When they've had a meal
- When they've been playing

He'll also go to the toilet when he feels his bladder or bowel are full – that may seem obvious, but please bear in mind that he has very little warning when he's a puppy. By the time he's realised he needs to go out, he's already going all over your carpet!

Have a very clear routine for taking your puppy to the area you've chosen for his toilet.

- First thing in the morning (don't wait to put the kettle on, go straight outside with him – **and stay with him** - no matter what the weather is doing, that's what umbrellas are for!).
- At least every hour during the day.
- At those other 'critical times' we've mentioned above.

You'll notice we urge you to go outside WITH HIM when he has urges of his own. This is because, if he feels isolated from the rest of his pack (you), he'll do everything in his power to come straight back in. The scratching on the door will convince you he's done what he needs to, and his relief at being back with the family will be expressed in entirely the wrong way!

Also, how can you tell him what a clever lad he is for going in the right place, if he's standing shivering on the doorstep and you're sitting inside with a cup of tea and the latest episode of Coronation Street?

Remember this is called 'houseTRAINING'. You can't train him if you're not with him!

We don't think it's a good idea to train a puppy to go to the toilet on newspaper as this just prolongs the agony. Newspaper is great for putting on the floor to make it easier to clean up housetraining mistakes, but look at this from his point of view ...

You may think you've trained him to go to the toilet on newspaper. Your puppy will just see the area – such as the kitchen – and think that's where he's supposed to go. Even when you remove the newspaper, the kitchen's still there and that's where he's always been praised for going to the toilet until now. Also, once you've trained a puppy to go to the toilet on newspaper, you will at some point have to re-train him not to.

Housetraining may take time, but be patient and eventually the penny will drop and he'll be spending pennies where you want him to.

Sometimes, when housetraining mistakes occur, it's easy to blame the puppy. However, yelling at your puppy or – even worse – physically punishing him (rubbing his nose in it, for example) will make matters much, much worse. If we had a quid for every owner who has punished their puppy and ended up with severe housetraining nightmares, we'd be millionaires.

Look at it this way – would you rub a baby's face in its nappy? No. We accept that human children will take years to 'housetrain' but we get really crabby with every single mistake a puppy makes. Get over it and get training!

If housetraining mistakes occur (they're YOUR mistakes – you weren't watching him closely enough) always clean up using either a special odour-eliminating product available from your vet or a mild solution of biological washing powder/liquid. Remember, if the accident was on carpet or soft furnishings, it's wise to do a colour fastness test first.

If things aren't going to plan, ask yourself the following questions:

- ✓ Have I been consistent and established a routine?
- ✓ Have I been going outside with my puppy to praise him when he gets it right?
- ✓ Have I watched him closely enough?
- ✓ Have I taken him outside often enough?
- ✓ Am I feeding a food that isn't suitable for him (e.g., if your puppy has regular bouts of diarrhoea, consult your vet)?

And lastly, if you bought your puppy from a puppy dealer (i.e., if you didn't see where the puppy was born and reared) he will probably have lived in squalid conditions. This means it may take a little longer to housetrain your puppy. However, follow the steps above, stick with it, and you will succeed.

CHEW CHEW TRAIN

Puppies chew for two reasons:
Firstly, they thoroughly enjoy it (they chew just as we'd sit down to read a good book or watch the telly). Secondly, they need to chew because teething makes their mouths sore. When babies cut their teeth they have sleepless nights, temperatures, and are prone to infections. Puppies will also be suffering.

Knowing that your puppy is going to chew, it seems sensible to 'chew train' him as early as possible.

He will chew anything he can sink his teeth into. Teach him what you'd prefer him to chew (safe toys such as Kongs or sterilised bones – see Stuff That Kong) and distract him with these safe items if you see him beginning to concentrate on a 'no-go' item.

Please bear in mind that he HAS to chew. He can do NOTHING about this.

Anything that is left within reach is fair game, so far as he's concerned. Remember what we said earlier about what's safe and dangerous? No matter how many times you tell him not to chew something, he'll forget all about it when you leave the room. So if your Italian leather shoes become open toe sandals because you left them on the coffee table – well, don't say we didn't warn you, and don't blame the puppy for your silliness.

STUFF THAT KONG!

1. Smear the inside of the Kong with something your puppy likes such as cream cheese, jam, peanut butter, or fish paste;
2. Stuff the Kong with either the puppy's own food, boiled rice, boiled pasta, or bread crusts;
3. Smear the opening of the Kong with whatever you've smeared around the inside to give the puppy a hint of the exciting things he'll find inside;
4. Stand well back and let battle commence!

SOCIALISATION & HABITUALISATION

Up until the age of about 14 weeks your puppy is like a sponge, soaking up new experiences. After that age, he will be reaching 'saturation' point and it will take longer for him to absorb anything new.

The older he gets, the more suspicious he will be of people and events that he has not already been exposed to.

So the clock is ticking to get your precious puppy out and about, meeting lots of different people and seeing lots of different things. If you dawdle, you've lost an opportunity that will not be offered again. This is a very short window of opportunity, so use it to the full!

N.B. Your puppy will be at risk from infections if you take him into public areas before his inoculation regime is completed. However, there's nothing to stop you carrying him or taking him on short car journeys. This protects him from possible infections, but introduces him to the outside world in a safe way.

Socialisation:

This is all about making sure your puppy will meet new people with confidence. He needs to meet toddlers, children, teenagers, adults, old people. He should also meet people of different ethnic groups. Aim at introducing him to ***at least TEN strangers every week,*** i.e., people he has never met before. He needs a massive circle of friends. Rope in your friends, neighbours, colleagues from work and their families. If you're a single female living alone, we would highly recommend getting lots of young men to visit. It's a tough job, but you've gotta do it!

Socialising your puppy with other dogs is also vital. He needs to meet sensible, calm adult dogs and/or other puppies that he can have pleasant experiences with and practice the all-important social skills that will keep him out of trouble in adulthood.

Puppies who have had a quiet social life often grow up to become wary of strangers and feel threatened or uncomfortable in their company.

Habitualisation:

You need your puppy to feel comfortable in lots of different situations and environments. So take this show on the road! You should start off with quieter places (such as the local shops) and progress as quickly as possible to places such as fairgrounds, railway and bus stations and the local pub. Take him on public transport so he becomes habituated to the different noises and smells. ***Be sensible with this;*** each puppy will be different. Monitor how comfortable he is in one situation before exposing him to other, more difficult situations. The more you do, the more he'll accept and he'll grow up into a confident, self-assured dog you can take anywhere. And what about introducing him to other animals, such as cats, pet-rabbits, chickens, sheep ... if you don't have any, find someone who does. It's far easier to introduce a puppy to these animals than a full-grown dog.

Be sensible when introducing your puppy to new people, objects, or environments. Monitor his reactions: is he confident, or does he seem worried? If he's worried ***do not comfort him!*** We know this sounds a little harsh, but puppies and dogs don't understand sympathy, but they DO understand that their anxieties have been noted and rewarded with a stroke and a gentle voice. If he seems worried, simply give him plenty of time and space to cope. NEVER make him 'face up to his fears'. Just be calm and confident and allow him to adjust in his own time.

Have a look at our 'Social Diary' at the back of the book. Be able to tick as many boxes as quickly as possible. ***Please*** do not think it is something that you can get round to when you have time.

N.B. Remember to ask your vet's advice on when it will be safe to mix him with other dogs or puppies.

HOW DO YOU DO?

Here are two very common problems. People complain about these all the time:

- My dog jumps up to say hello
- My dog is aggressive to people delivering the post/milk/newspaper, etc.

These may seem two very different problems, but both can be prevented very simply by the puppy's family giving the puppy the correct information about how to behave from the moment they bring him home.

We've talked briefly about jumping up in our 'How Puppies Learn' section, but let's go into it in more detail here.

Puppies greet older members of a canine pack by licking around their muzzles. When your puppy meets someone, his natural instinct is to try to get to their face, hence they jump up. As we saw in 'How Puppies Learn', admonishing the puppy will not have the desired result. You need to teach your puppy an alternative to jumping up that will please everyone.

Teach your puppy to sit, using kind, reward based methods that your socialisation class will show you. Teach him to sit in the kitchen, the living room, the yard, the front garden, by the gate, at the side of the kerb ... this will teach him to sit in lots of different situations. Now, when your puppy comes to greet you, ask him to 'sit' and reward him with your attention when he does. Make sure EVERYONE he meets asks him to sit before rewarding him. It will soon become a habit for him to sit when he's saying hello.

Now for the second problem ... Your puppy will grow up to be an adult who behaves instinctively to protect his territory. Regular visitors such as postal workers, etc., are people he never actually meets and makes friends with. At some point, he will bark at them when they come to the front door and they will beat a hasty retreat. He thinks, 'Hurrah! If it weren't for me, that intruder would have broken in!' He doesn't know they were going anyway.

Pretty soon, he'll be waking you up in the early hours because he can hear the milkman coming down the street. Pretty soon, he'll be shredding the newspaper as it lands on the mat. Pretty soon, the Post Office will be instructing you to collect your mail as they're tired of being threatened by your dog when they try to deliver it.

What can we do to prevent this problem? We can ***introduce*** him to all these people when he's still a baby puppy. They can give him a biscuit and a fuss (and, of course, you can ask them to make sure he sits before they say hello) and he'll come to look forward to their visit. As he grows, why not take it a step further, and teach him to retrieve the post and the paper?

So there you have it: two very common problems and two very simple ways to ***prevent it happening in the first place!!*** Please, please give your puppy the opportunity to learn the correct way to behave. If you neglect his education, we will gain no satisfaction at all from saying, 'We told you so.'

THE INDOOR KENNEL – YOUR PUP'S OWN BEDSIT

Indoor kennels are a great asset when you've a new puppy. These are a 'home within a home' that provide your puppy with security, and you with peace of mind!

Some people mistakenly think indoor kennels can be cruel because they look like a cage. However, no one would think of leaving a toddler alone with access to boiling kettles, electricity sockets and other dangerous items so they put him in a play-pen. An indoor kennel is just a 'puppy play-pen'. ***Your puppy deserves the same security*** when you can't watch him or if you have to leave him while you nip quickly to the shops, for instance.

Indoor kennels should only be used for short periods of time (a maximum of 2 hours), though they can be used overnight as your puppy should be sleeping anyway. It would be counter-productive to use the indoor kennel as a 'sin bin' to send your puppy when you think he's been misbehaving (shouldn't you be training him, rather than punishing him?) as it should be somewhere he feels secure and content. It should not be the canine equivalent of the coal shed!!

Should your puppy ever need to spend time at the vets or a grooming parlour, he will be placed in an indoor kennel. Imagine how much happier he'll be if he is already used to this mode of accommodation?

You need to teach the puppy what the indoor kennel is for. Unless the breeder has been using them correctly, this is the first time he will have seen one. Start off by putting the indoor kennel where you intend your puppy to sleep. At various times, encourage the puppy into the indoor kennel by placing a treat or a chew inside. At this point, do not close the door on the puppy as we don't want him to feel trapped before he's had a chance to get used to the space. Leave the puppy's bed inside and allow him to sleep in the indoor kennel whenever he's tired but again, leave the door open so he has free access.

Once you see your puppy choosing to rest in the indoor kennel (partly covering the kennel with a towel or blanket can help create the impression of a 'den') you can place a long-lasting chew or a stuffed kong inside for the puppy to chew. Quietly close the door for a couple of minutes. He might not even be aware he's been shut in! Do this four to five times per day and you will be able to leave him inside with the door closed in quite a short period of time (probably two to three days – though each puppy is different).

Remember not to inadvertently reward unwanted behaviour. If your puppy is barking to be let out, wait until he has gone quiet again before opening the door, and realise that you probably asked for too much too soon. If your puppy thinks that by barking he can get you to do what he wants, you may be storing up a whole heap of trouble!

Of course, if your puppy is really distressed you should open up immediately so you can check he is alright, but the chances of this happening will be very rare if you have followed the instructions carefully and made certain that you aren't pushing him too fast.

When buying an indoor kennel, make sure you buy one that will be large enough to comfortably accommodate your puppy when he is fully grown. When an adult, he should be able to sit upright without hitting his head, be able to turn around without turning himself inside out, and be able to lie stretched out without any of his paws touching the bars. If in doubt, buy the biggest you can!

'DON'T LEAVE ME THIS WAY!'

Puppies get into a lot of trouble when they're on their own. Some of it will be related to boredom, frustration, and anxiety; and some of it will be related to phases the puppy is going through, such as teething troubles.

Whatever is causing the problem, it is important to recognise that your puppy is not doing this on purpose or to spite you. They do it for any number of reasons, but getting back at you for leaving them on their own is not one of them.

WHAT'S SAFE & DANGEROUS

We talked about this in 'How Puppies Learn'. If there's no one to distract your puppy or tell him not to, he thinks it's okay to rip up the carpet or dismantle the TV remote control. This is often the problem with puppies who need to chew to keep their jaws from aching, and have not yet learned that some things are not appropriate.

No one knows why puppies chew the TV remote, but pups everywhere do it. Who knows, maybe he's a Neighbours fan and was trying to catch the early afternoon show? Or maybe he is trying to tell you something far more fundamental...

BOREDOM

Imagine sitting for hours on end with no telly to watch, no radio to listen to, no book to read, no crossword to complete. You'd go just a little crazy, wouldn't you? Now remember your pup is in the same position every day when you're at work. Is it any wonder he has to amuse himself? Puppies chew instinctively to keep their teeth and jaws in good working order. And with nothing better to do, who can blame them?

ANXIETY

As pack animals, dogs really aren't happy being left alone. It's not natural for dogs in the same way that it is for cats that are happy to cat-nap for hours.

For some puppies, being left in solitary confinement can be very distressing and they do their best to escape: they might dig up the carpet by the door where you left, or they take things that hold your scent and lie on them, just to give them a little comfort.

Other things can worry your pup during your absence: perhaps children tease them through the letter box, or someone knocks on your door. All these things can upset him and encourage him to partake in something called 'displacement activity' – in other words, something to take his mind off whatever is worrying him. This normally takes the form of chewing and tearing things.

Don't scold your pup when you arrive home to shredded belongings – you may just be adding to his anxiety. If he is suffering from this problem, remember to leave nothing of value in a place that he can reach: if your mobile phone or credit-card-packed wallet becomes the latest victim of bored jaws – IT'S YOUR FAULT!

<u>WHAT YOU CAN DO</u>

First of all, don't punish your pup if you come home to a disaster. Research has shown that unless you either reward or punish a behaviour within half a second, a dog cannot make a connection between the action and it's consequence. So if your pup destroyed the settee cushions within half an hour of you leaving, he won't make the connection between those cushions and your scolding when you return five hours later. It just makes for a miserable hound that can't understand why you've suddenly turned nasty. Now he's anxious about being alone and anxious about your return and yes, the soft furnishings will suffer even more as a result! Whose fault? YOURS!

Practise makes perfect. Get your pup used to being on his own for short periods and build up gradually. Don't make a big fuss of him when you leave him, just calmly walk out the door and return within a couple of minutes. If he has started whining, wait until he has stopped or he will think his whining brought you back and this could start a problem with him barking all day to call you home. After all, barking does work because, as far as he is concerned, you do always eventually come home!

When dogs in the wild have been resting and want to go hunting, they wake each other up, chatter and groom each other before setting off together. This is why it's important to make sure you don't give your dog the wrong signals by getting him excited just before you leave. You need to reduce the contrast between when you're there and when you're not.

So cut out the 'Bye bye lickle hunny-bunny; mummy won't be long ...'

Enrich your puppy's environment. Give your puppy something to think about while you're gone. Leave a stuffed Kong or two for him to chew on (rather than the furniture), and what about putting his dried food in a Buster Cube to help keep his attention off the rug. Why not leave some treats hidden around the house for him to discover? All these things will take his mind off his solitude and give him something positive to think about. Although it may not take a lot of energy, using his brain in these ways will make him physically tired. If he regularly chooses the rug as a chew toy, why not roll it up and put it out of his way until you can trust him?

Invest in an indoor kennel. Indoor kennels really are a very worthwhile purchase if you are only going to leave your pup for a couple of hours, or if you have problems overnight.

Don't expect too much. If your puppy is left alone all day, expect to have problems! His bladder and bowels will not be able to last that long and he may have no choice but to soil inside the house. Boredom will also be a major factor for a bright, inquisitive puppy. Arrange for relatives, friends, neighbours or dog-sitters to visit your puppy during the day to alleviate these problems.

PUPPIES AND CHILDREN – AN IDEAL COMBINATION?

Research has shown that children raised with pets grow up to be healthier and more rounded individuals. Pet ownership gives them a sense of responsibility and teaches them a lot about life in general.

So that's what a puppy could do for your child – what could your child do for your puppy? Some breeds are said to be 'good with children' but what the breeders really mean is that they'll put up with more punishment before they snap. The bull breeds such as Staffordshire Bull Terriers and Bullmastiffs are also supposed to be good with children. Why is this? Because they have a high pain threshold. What does this say about how some adults allow children to handle puppies?

A puppy will be the ideal playmate for a child – ***but only if some ground rules are set from the beginning.*** We're not going to talk about how the puppy should behave around the child, we're going to concentrate on how the child should behave with the puppy! This is because, unless your child behaves in the correct way, your puppy has a life of pain and misery ahead of him and, should he ever object to mistreatment, he'll be labelled as aggressive and unpredictable and a one-way trip to the vet is the likely outcome.

So ***children must be taught to RESPECT the puppy*** as a living, breathing animal capable of feeling pain, as well as love. Do not allow a child to pick up a puppy, unless you would trust that same child to hold a human baby. Involve the children in training the puppy using the methods we've described. Games and playtime are great, but make sure they are always supervised. Rough and tumble games, in particular, can lead to either puppy or child becoming over-excited and that always ends in tears! Involve your children in the day-to-day care of the puppy, including clearing up after him, and you'll teach your children that those we love are worth the effort.

If you don't have children, it's important that your puppy should meet nice, sensible children so that he can learn that children are fun to be around. If your puppy doesn't meet children, he may grow up to fear them. Children don't behave in the same way as adults; they have high, squeaky voices, they're noisy and unpredictable, and all those things can cause even an adult dog to react badly. So time is ticking on ... borrow some children while your puppy is still young and teach your puppy that all humans, young and old, are their friends.

SOMETHING TO SINK YOUR TEETH INTO!

At the moment your puppy still has his razor sharp, hypodermic teeth. He will be shedding these teeth soon to make way for bigger, stronger teeth that will be capable of gripping and tearing at flesh. Now isn't that a sobering thought!

Pups have sharp milk teeth to encourage their mother to introduce the pups to solid food (well would you like those things clamping onto your most tender parts?). Suddenly, it's no fun to let them feed off her and she starts to avoid them when they try to suckle. This is all part of the growing process for the pups who, up until this moment, have probably never been denied anything. This introduces them to the feeling of frustration and how to cope with it.

However, another part of this growing process is that playing with their litter-mates becomes more painful. Rather than giving a powerful suck, their teeth can inflict a painful, if harmless, pressure. Litter-mates tell the biting pup in no uncertain terms that this is not acceptable. They'll squeal in pain and refuse to play. This teaches the pup to inhibit his bite so that it isn't exerting as much pressure. If he doesn't, no one will play with him.

Copying the behaviour of his litter-mates and mother will help your pup understand that his teeth are hurting you. Human skin is far more fragile than dog's and, while he thinks that the playful mouthing is gentle, you may have other ideas!

So what should you do when your pup is mouthing? Well, to make it easy for him to understand, why not continue the education already begun when he was with his mother and litter-mates? You should cry out (as though mortally wounded!) then walk away from the puppy. You might even need to leave the room, closing the door behind you. The puppy will soon realise that, when he uses his teeth, the fun and games stop and he's left in the room alone. Don't make the mistake of trying to catch him so that you can put HIM outside ... he'll just learn that biting you is a prelude to a wonderfully exciting game of chase!

Now you'll always get some know-all at work who'll tell you that you should hit your pup on the nose if he mouths. This does not work and will either make your pup shy away from your hand or learn to bite harder because he's suddenly not playing but fighting back! If the person who gives you this bad advice is a colleague then tell him he's way behind the times (if he's your boss, of course, you should ignore his advice but tell him it worked!).

Mouthing will decrease in time but it won't stop overnight. Using these methods will, however, speed up the process.

YOUR PUPPY'S NAME

Your puppy's name should mean 'Look at me because something nice is going to happen.' So many puppies learn their name means they're in trouble and they'd better make themselves scarce. No wonder, then, that when you call their name in the park the puppy isn't so keen to come back!

Trips to the park are very exciting for your puppy – if you've done a good job of socialising him he'll be interested in everything that's going on and be confident enough to explore. However, initially he'll want to keep close to you because he's not as confident as he will be when he matures. This is the perfect time to be playing recall games.

All of these games can be practised in the house, a secure garden, or the park.

'Puppy in the Middle'

What you'll need: two or more people, one puppy, and lots of treats. Unlike 'Piggy in the middle', your puppy will win every time. Call him between the two of you and, when he arrives at each person, they should put a finger in his collar (to stop him doing the fast food trick of snack and run) and then give him a treat. Once one person has fed him, the next person can call him and so on. Each time he goes to the person who's called him, he'll get a reward and have great fun.

'Hide and Seek'

An extension of 'Puppy in the Middle'. One person hides while the other holds the pup. Make it easy to start off with by letting the puppy see where the other person has gone. Now the person who is hiding calls the puppy and the puppy races off after them. Again, a finger in the collar precedes the treat. When he's got the idea of the game, don't let him see where the person has hidden and let him search them out. Again, this can be practised just as effectively in the house as the park.

Because these games can be played in the house and secure garden, ***there's no reason to wait until his inoculations have finished.*** Practise now and you'll have established a really good habit to use later on when he's able to visit the local park.

GETTING YOUR PUPPY USED TO THE LEAD

As with so much in life, wearing a collar and lead is not natural for a puppy! It'll take him a little while to get used to the idea, but we can do lots of things to make the transition more comfortable for him and less of a struggle for you.

Choose a lightweight collar and let your puppy wear it at times when he's going to be distracted by something he enjoys doing, such as eating and playing. This means the collar will be on for short periods initially but the time can be built up gradually. By the time you've had your puppy for a couple of weeks he should be happy to wear the collar.

Even with this gradual approach, the puppy will still scratch and worry at his collar. This is normal and he should not get any attention for doing it. Just carry on with what you were doing (preparing his food or playing with him) and he'll soon forget about it.

NEVER leave the collar on the puppy when he's going to be alone. He might get the collar caught on something and injure himself by trying to get free.

Once he's happy with his collar, you can introduce his lead. Again, a lightweight lead is recommended. Leave this trailing along behind him at those 'special' times, such as feeding and playtime, and he'll soon forget the lead is there.

Now comes the tricky bit! Start picking up the lead and encouraging the puppy to come with you. If he struggles, drop the lead so that he doesn't panic (obviously, this is done in the house or a secure garden where he can't run away if you drop the lead). Pick up the lead again and keep trying. You may need a piece of his dried food or a toy to entice him along.

Once he's happy with the lead and no longer panics, you can go onto the next level of collar and lead training. As your puppy walks along with you, pay attention to make sure that he isn't rewarded for pulling on the lead. What do we mean? Well, if he pulls to get somewhere and you follow like a good little owner, what are you teaching him? Of course! You're teaching him to pull on the lead! Not such a problem now, but wait until he's an eight stone adult! Even a pulling Yorkshire Terrier can be a problem during icy weather.

So if he pulls on the lead you must stop. Encourage him to come back to you and then carry on walking. ***You never ever EVER follow him when he's pulling on the lead.***

By training your puppy in this way, he'll be a delight to take for a walk – rather than him taking you!

PURE IN MIND AND BODY!

Your puppy will need two types of exercise – physical and mental. Without providing him with ways of burning off his physical and mental energy, you run the risk of having a puppy who is bored beyond belief. This can quickly turn into behavioural problems and even result in mental illness.

Physical exercise in a puppy is not an exact science, but you should pay heed to what your veterinary surgeon advises. ***Too much physical exercise can be as harmful as too little.***

Mental exercise, however, has no such boundaries but is equally as important!! ***Through fun-training and appropriate games your puppy will receive mental stimulation which prevents boredom. A bored puppy makes up its own games ... take it from us: you won't enjoy them!***

Charities such as Canine Partners for Independence start training their puppies when they are just 7 weeks old. By the time your puppy has finished his inoculations and is able to join Puppy Socialisation Classes he's a mature student by their standards! His brain wave patterns are faster now than they will be when he gets older (well, we all slow down, don't we?).

So the old saying 'You can't teach an old dog new tricks', while not strictly true, does have some basis in fact.

You may have heard that you shouldn't start training a puppy until it is six months old. This was because training methods in the past involved choke chains and physically pushing puppies into position. Until a puppy was six months old he would be unable to cope – either physically or mentally! Indeed, many puppies were so often too traumatised by the methods used that they would be deemed 'untrainable' and either given away or put to sleep.

Training your puppy should be light-hearted and involve a lot of laughter and love. It should be fun for both of you. Don't train your puppy when you aren't feeling at your brightest or if you're in a mood. You're probably not fun to be with at times like this, so why put your pup through that? His eyes should light up at the thought of training, not be raised to heaven!

Your Socialisation Class trainers will be able to give you lots of ideas for training that will keep things fun for both of you.

CHOOSING A PUPPY CLASS

Did you know that your puppy's brain waves are faster than an adult dog's? That's because they are learning so much all the time. ***Make sure they're learning the right stuff!***

A well-run puppy class is lots of fun. But how can you tell if the class you've chosen will be of value to you and your puppy? Here are some special points for consideration before you join:

- ❖ Always go to see the classes first to ensure the trainer uses kind methods.
- ❖ It should be a special class for puppies only (under 20 weeks) as badly behaved adult dogs can scare puppies or teach them the bad habits they've already learned.
- ❖ Ideally, it should be run by a member of the Association of Pet Dog Trainers (APDT). Members of the APDT won't allow choke chains or harsh methods.
- ❖ There should be no more than five puppies per trainer. If there are more than that, are you getting value for money?
- ❖ If there is free play, is it controlled and sensible, or a free-for-all that could result in injured or frightened puppies?
- ❖ Has all the family been encouraged to attend (including well-behaved children)?
- ❖ The class should consist of basic obedience exercises, socialisation, with everyone in the class being involved and having fun.
- ❖ If something they've suggested isn't working, does the trainer listen to you and help, or dismiss your worries as irrelevant?

Beware of the poorly run puppy class:

- ❖ The class is a mixture of puppies and older dogs who may already have bad habits or even have behaviour problems. This will not be a safe, fun environment for your sensitive pup!
- ❖ Off-lead play is really a 'free-for-all' where some puppies learn to be bullies and others become victims. The bullies learn that playing with other dogs is far more fun than listening to their owner. The victims don't enjoy any part of the process!

- ❖ Harsh training methods may be used. Are choke chains recommended? These instruments of torture are old-fashioned and dangerous.
- ❖ Owners who ask questions are ignored, dismissed, or even ridiculed.
- ❖ Only one person is allowed to train the puppy. This reduces the opportunity for the whole family to be involved with the training.

Puppy classes are often run by the Club's novice trainer as a 'practise run' for the 'real work'. These well-meaning people may be very pleasant but lack the expertise and knowledge to run these specialised courses. Puppies are cute and cuddly, but a good trainer can spot potential problems, even at a very young age, and give advice accordingly. Problems spotted in a young puppy can be resolved much more quickly. After all, prevention is better than cure!

<u>This is the most important time in your puppy's life.</u> A good class is worth seeking out, even if it means extra travel. Good training classes are hard to find but well worth it!

WHAT'S yours IS MINE AND WHAT'S mines MY OWN!!

Your puppy will instinctively feel that he should acquire and keep anything of value. In the wild, this would be represented by a part of the kill. In domestic situations, valuable items include his dinner, his toys, and anything he learns that you find valuable!

The Food Bowl Blues

Watching wolf packs, it's interesting to see that even the lowest member of the pack will defend its dinner against the higher-ranking members. The higher-ranking members accept this and back away. No one wants a fight that may result in damage to any wolf in the pack. That prat who tells you to 'show the dog who's boss' will almost certainly tell you that taking your puppy's food away from him while he's eating will do the trick. ***It won't!*** If even high-ranking members of the pack understand canine etiquette, what will your puppy think of you? He'll think you're rude beyond belief but, if he tries to tell you off, you become aggressive. Now he thinks – what sort of people am I living with? They have no manners, and when I object to their bullying tactics they get even worse. He'd better defend himself, hadn't he? After all, he has no idea what you'll try next!

Can you see how easy it would be to totally undermine your relationship with your puppy over such a silly misunderstanding?

It's still important, though, to be able to handle your puppy's food while he's eating. After all, there may be children in the house or that visit, who don't understand these canine rules, or maybe at some point you need to move his food for some reason. We need to teach him that humans around his food bowl mean good news. Here's how we're going to do it:

- From the first day your puppy comes home, set aside some really tasty morsels to add to his food bowl while he's eating. Drop them in there as he's munching to show him that you are a good person to have around while he's eating.
- Once he's really comfortable with this, ask other people in the household to do the same.

- The last stage is to ask the children to do this (under supervision, obviously).

This is the way to prevent a problem occurring. If you have an older puppy, you should take the above steps more slowly, ensuring that your puppy is relaxed and happy before progressing to another stage. Danger signals to watch out for are that the puppy pauses in its chewing, but remains standing over its food with its mouth hovering just above the food bowl. Or if the puppy remains eating, but starts eating even more quickly. Both of these are signs that the puppy is not yet happy to move onto the next stage. These are quite subtle signs to watch out for but, unfortunately, dogs are far more subtle in their communication than stupid humans have given them credit for. It's only due to recent, ground-breaking research that we're even scraping the surface when it comes to how dogs communicate.
Obviously, if your puppy pauses in eating because he's rushing over to you with a happy, wagging tail, or if he stopped eating but is looking up at you expectantly, these are signs that the pup is so happy with your presence that he feels confident enough to leave his food. This is just what we'd hope for.

'Chase me, Chase me!'

What about items other than food in his bowl? Puppies are exploring their environment all the time. They experiment with things by picking them up and chewing them (just like a baby would). They want to know if it's alive, is it edible, will it make a good toy? So far as he's concerned, anything that's left around the house that he can reach is up for grabs. And grabbing is just what he'll do.

Now what is he to think when he takes hold of an item and suddenly finds the family rushing round after him? Does he think:

1. Oops, I'd better let go of this
2. Wow! What a brilliant game!
3. Hang on, this must be really valuable, therefore I should defend it at all costs

Sorry, he's unlikely to think Option One, and more likely to think Option 2 or 3.

Now let's say that he's taken something and you're all running around after him (great game!). Then, one of you manages to corner and grab him and wrestle with him to retrieve the 'toy' (he doesn't know it's a £20 note, after all). Now it's getting a little more serious, isn't it? What started off as a game has become a little bit scary. His tender mouth may even be hurt by the rough handling. Once again, you're in danger of teaching this puppy that he should be wary of you and should defend himself.

What can we do, then, to help the puppy learn the difference between what's acceptable and what isn't?

1. Give him lots of toys he CAN chew on. (See our special section on Chew Training).
2. Make sure that anything you don't want him to have is removed from his reach. If he gets it, think about whether it's something you can sacrifice and leave him to it.

3. If it's something too important to become a chew toy, don't chase after him and risk turning this into a fun game. Instead, tell him what a clever boy he is, go to one of his chew toys and start playing with it. He will probably come to investigate what you're playing with. If he does, have a game with him and calmly retrieve the precious item and place it out of reach.

The trick here is to redirect his attention onto something appropriate, without teaching him that if he pinches something then you'll start to play a game with him. That's why it's important to make sure that this is something that happens very rarely indeed – so keep the house tidy while you have a puppy! And if you have kids, what better way to teach them to put their toys away than having the puppy remodel them into little bits!! It might sound like a good way to have house-proud children, but can your puppy's digestive system cope with little bits of Barbie or Action Man floating through his small intestine?

Perhaps this aspect of your puppy's behaviour is the best demonstration of how much he still resembles his wolf ancestry? While we may think that a dropped paper handkerchief needs retrieving so he won't shred it and cause a mess on the carpet, your puppy has a very different view of the situation! Because you feel it is so important, he may begin to view ALL paper hankies as so high in value that he should resist all attempts to retrieve it!

It may be hard to believe, but there are very many dogs in people's homes who become 'untrustworthy and unpredictable' when a hankie or piece of paper flutters to the floor. This is because their owners have failed to understand the different way their canine friend has interpreted human behaviour.

Don't fall into the same trap. Follow these simple guidelines and peace will reign in your household.

CAR TRAVEL

The first trip your puppy took in a car was probably to come home with you. It will have been stressful, exciting, and probably vomit inducing!

Therefore, we need to teach the puppy to cope with the excitement or anxiety of being in a car. ***It will be important that he takes lots of short trips*** to help him realise that they don't always end either at the vet's or the park.

Ensure you take your puppy for these short journeys when his stomach is fairly empty. The best place for him to travel is in a specially designed car cage (if you have a hatchback or estate vehicle). This will keep him secure and prevent him being a dangerous distraction. It will also ensure that he can't escape from the car if you open a door for any reason.

Another excellent method of containing your pup while in the car is with a special seat-belt harness available at good pet shops. Puppies are in danger of injury during a crash just as unsecured adults or children are. Even a low impact crash can have a devastating effect if your puppy is thrown through the windscreen or against a hard surface. As with the car crate, your puppy cannot distract you from your driving, or escape through an open door.

You should also ***be sure that your puppy cannot escape through an open window.*** Driving while allowing your puppy to lean out through a window is incredibly stupid! In a crash he would almost certainly be hurled from the vehicle, he could escape if he saw something that caught his interest, or he could be injured by road chippings flying up from the wheels of the car in front of you.

Take time to consider your puppy's safety while in the car. By keeping him secure in either a car crate or a seat harness, you can relax in the knowledge that he is as safe as you can make him. Now all you have to worry about is the idiots driving around you!

If your puppy is regularly car sick, make sure that trips are kept short and unexciting. If the problem persists, you could ask your vet for car-sickness remedies.

Ensuring that your puppy is safe and relaxed will mean your canine companion can travel with you on lots of exciting journeys.

N.B. ***Dogs die in hot cars.*** They become over-heated very quickly and dehydrate. Death follows quickly. Dogs have higher body temperatures than humans so that even moderate temperatures can be lethal. DO NOT LEAVE YOUR PUPPY OR ADULT DOG IN THE CAR. Always carry fresh water and a drinking bowl. Even a traffic jam on a motorway could cause problems if he cannot stay cool.

GROOMING & HANDLING

Even if you have a short coated dog, such as a boxer or a labrador, grooming and handling must be part of your daily routine.

It's very important to have a puppy who grows into a dog that enjoys being groomed and handled. It makes them far easier to live with, groom, and take to the vet. Grooming is part of the bonding process, and dogs in a pack will often groom each other when they are feeling relaxed and secure. By grooming and handling your puppy you will, therefore, make him feel the same – part of a loving family.

Trying to groom the puppy while he's having his 'mad half hour' is totally counter productive! During these rushes of adrenalin and energy he'll find it impossible to sit still and will make the whole exercise a waste of time.

It is important that the grooming and handling is a pleasant experience for your puppy. Children must not handle the puppy roughly; he is not a fluffy toy! Be sure you have thoroughly read our section on Puppies and Children.

Grooming should not be a power struggle or a wrestling match. The easiest way to teach your puppy to enjoy being groomed is by waiting until he is relaxed, then feeding the biting end with treats, while gently grooming and running your hands over the rest of his body. We recommend 'Zoom Grooms', which are available at most good pet shops. Zoom Grooms are made of rubber and are very gentle. They massage the skin as well as getting rid of an amazing amount of shed hair! They are easy to clean and suit the majority of coat types, the exception being woolly-coated breeds such as Bichon Frise, Poodle, and Bedlington Terrier. Speak to the breeder about the best grooming tool for this type of breed.

You should also concentrate on those parts of the puppy's body which will need attention later on. These areas include his tail, ears, mouth, paws, skin, and tummy. If you have a particularly strong stomach, ensure he is happy to be investigated around genitals and anal glands.

Gently investigate these areas as part of your daily routine. The best time to do this is just before you feed him – because then you have his full attention. By handling him quietly and sensibly every day you will be able to tell when there's something bothering him physically. Maybe one day he shies away when you try to look in his ears? Perhaps he's not so keen to let you look at his paws? ***Daily handling and grooming is part of your 'early warning system'*** and, by nipping the problem in the bud, your vets fees will be kept to a minimum.

HEALTH AND WELFARE

Your puppy needs good quality dog food, fresh water, and a draught free bed. Those are all the requirements he needs to keep him alive. But they alone will not keep him happy.

So what else does he need? He needs companionship, lots of regular trips to a toilet area, mental and physical exercise, a secure pack, and understanding owners. We've covered all of these elements in different sections, but without all of them together he will be sadly lacking important components in his life. The lack of just one of these will have a negative impact on the others.

Your vet is the best person to talk to about your puppy's health. He or she is your first port of call – not your neighbour who's owned dogs for years, or the bloke in work who 'knows what he's talking about' because, unless they have the letters MRCVS after their names they won't know as much as your vet!

Veterinary attention is costly. There is no NHS for your pet. Advances in medical science means that all sorts of treatments are now available. Invest in **health insurance** for your pup. There are many insurance companies who are desperate for your custom so pick carefully. Talk to your vet about companies they recommend. They'll have lots of experience dealing with different companies and know which company will pay out and which rely on small print to wriggle out of the claim. Also, some insurance policies only pay out for an illness for one year. These policies may seem cheaper, but if your pet suffers from a chronic disorder then you're in trouble! Some disorders may mean your puppy needs treatment for the rest of his life (such as heart disease). Imagine how awful it would be to have to put your puppy to sleep because you could no longer afford to keep him healthy?

We recommend **permanent identification** for your puppy, in case he gets lost or is stolen. A collar with a tag is the easiest way to ensure your pup is returned to you, but collars can fall off or be removed. We recommend that you have your pup identified with a **microchip,** or a **tattoo** – or both! Then, if your pet does stray, you can advertise that he is permanently identified in this way. All of this will make it more likely that your pup is returned quickly and with the minimum fuss.

If your puppy should get loose or go missing during a walk, contact the local RSPCA, dog wardens, and police stations immediately. Go through the Yellow Pages for the telephone numbers of small, independent rescue kennels and visit them with a photo of your puppy or a detailed description. It is a legal requirement that, when in public, your puppy is wearing a collar with an identity tag containing your details.

OWNING MORE THAN ONE DOG

People often think that owning more than one dog is twice the fun but half the work; after all, they'll amuse themselves, won't they? However, although it can be great fun it is at least four times harder! Dogs never learn the right things from each other. If you have an older dog with 99 good habits and one bad habit, you can bet any money you like that your new puppy will learn that one bad habit!

Left to its own devices, the puppy in a multi-dog household will bond more closely to another canine because they share the same interests, have the same hobbies, and speak the same language. You must work hard to ensure that both dogs see you as the best thing in their lives.

Treat each pet as an individual and spend quality time with them. You should walk them separately so they learn to stand on their own four paws, feed them separately so they never become jealous about the food the other is eating. They should also sleep separately so that they can cope with being on their own should something happen to their canine companion.

Playing with and training your pets individually is even more important. They'll love playing together but they need to see their relationship with you as more important than the relationship they have with each other. Playing and training are such crucial parts in establishing and maintaining a good rapport with your puppy that it is essential it is taken seriously – especially if you are already competing for his affection!

Let's look at some problems that will occur if your dogs spend too much time together and not enough time with you:

- They become obsessed with each other but couldn't give a hoot about you. Training them becomes a nightmare and they cause endless mischief.
- Don't believe that, because they're brother and sister, they won't make even more mischief! The patter of tiny paws can occur even in the closest of families! Consider neutering them both, to ensure this can't happen.

❖ They enjoy lots of rough and tumble play-times and think other dogs in the park will enjoy it too. They can't understand when other dogs object and may start becoming fearful or aggressive.

Owning more than one dog doesn't seem like such an easy ride now, does it!!

The same rules apply if your puppy spends a lot of his time with a canine pal from another household.

We don't mean to sound as though every household that owns more than one dog is heading for disaster, owning more than one dog can be incredibly rewarding, ***but only if you are prepared to invest the necessary time and effort.***

THE LAW AND ITS IMPLICATIONS

The law and implications

Ask your local council for a copy of its bye-laws relating to dogs. You may be inadvertently breaking some of the rules! For instance, it will be illegal to walk your dog near a road without a collar and lead. The collar should have a tag with your details on, should your puppy become lost. This is part of national law.

It is the height of stupidity to walk a dog near a road without it being under the control of a leash. Your puppy may be very well-behaved, but at no stage will he be trustworthy enough to risk his life. What if a cat ran out in front of him? Perhaps another dog might run out of a gateway and attack him? Would he be startled if a car back-fired? These are just a few examples of things that can go wrong. Use your imagination and you'll be able to think of dozens of others. It isn't worth the risk.

Laws controlling dogs can be very severe. The Dangerous Dogs Act came into force following some horrific attacks by Pit Bull Terriers who had not been properly trained or socialised. ***Did you know, however, that the same Act of Parliament covers ALL breeds of dog, not just Pit Bulls?*** If your puppy runs up to someone who is frightened of dogs, and that person believes your puppy is dangerous, they can report you to the police for having a dangerous dog. Your puppy need not have bitten, snapped, growled, or even barked. He may have raced towards them with a wagging tail but, if you're frightened of dogs, this will make no difference. So be aware of other people and understanding of their possible fears. Teach your puppy from the moment you get him that, while other people are nice to meet, he should return to you as soon as you call him.

Walking your puppy in the countryside can be great fun, once he is old enough to walk any distance. Once again, be aware of other people and, this time, their livelihoods. Sheep are very inviting to chase and, though your puppy may mean them no harm, the sheep won't know that! Sheep are quite fragile creatures in some respects and running around a field carrying a full fleece on those spindly legs can mean they will suffer heart failure up to 30 minutes after the chase has ended. Sheep with lambs, on the other hand, may not turn and run but turn and face your puppy. Close to, sheep are surprisingly big and will attack your puppy if they feel their lambs are in danger.

Don't walk in a field with cattle who have calves. Just like sheep, cows can be very protective and may attack a puppy. If you get in the way, or if they see you as part of the attack, they may kill you.

Farmers are, by law, allowed to shoot dead any dog they see worrying their livestock. And the word 'worrying' should be read in its literal sense. Your puppy does not need to be actually attacking the livestock, he could be chasing them out of a sense of fun. The farmer knows how much danger his stock is in, however, and will respond accordingly.

The moral of the story is to be very aware of how the arrival of your puppy may impact on the lives of others. Don't assume everyone will love him and understand what a friendly chap he is! Make sure you train him well, using the techniques we've described, and be considerate of others. In this way, you're more likely to make people smile when your puppy appears, and he'll be welcome wherever he goes.

PUPPY PROOF YOUR HOME

With children, we take steps to ensure chubby fingers can't get into plug sockets; unsteady feet can't take the tumbling toddler upstairs; and all sorts of devices come into play to keep the child safe.

Your puppy needs the same consideration. He's a baby, exploring his environment and has no idea what might be dangerous or poisonous. Get down on your hands and knees (close the curtains, your neighbours don't need this sort of entertainment) and look at things from his point of view.

Plants, ornaments, electricity cables: they'll be 'explored'. While this can be annoying for you, it could be lethal for your puppy. Listed below are some items that could do far more harm to your puppy than you might have realised.

The Kitchen

The litter bin may contain broken glass, brittle meat bones, sharp cans, empty household cleaner bottles, etc. Move the bin to somewhere your puppy can't reach it, such as a work surface.

Floor level kitchen cupboards/fridge. While left alone, might he work out how to open the cupboards. What would he find inside? Buy some child-proof locks to make sure he can't gain access.

The Living Room

Electricity cables might get bitten through and electrocute your puppy. Cover them up.

Ornaments can get chewed and small pieces swallowed. Move them.

Audio and video tapes: if swallowed these long lines unravel in the gut and can take hours for a veterinary surgeon to remove during a very costly operation. How costly? It could cost the puppy his life.

Remote controls: The 'Fisher Price' of the puppy's toys! They love them! Again, sharp pieces swallowed could be lethal, but an even bigger concern is the batteries they contain - these are powered by extremely toxic chemicals.

Houseplants: some houseplants are toxic, or the soil they stand in might contain items such as slow-release fertilisers. Alternatively, the leaves may have been sprayed with pesticides.

The Garden, Garage and Shed

Are there any gaps in your fence through which a puppy can escape? Check behind the shrubs as your puppy will spot places you wouldn't normally see.

Soil improvers, fertilisers, and pesticides must be used with extreme care. Check the can, what does it say about pets? If you've just got your puppy, have you used these things recently? Is he safe to prowl among the shrubs and plants?

Slug pellets can be fatal if ingested. The easiest way to avoid this is to stop using them. Don't worry about the slugs eating your plants, your puppy will 'prune' them anyway!

Antifreeze stored in the garage is a very sweet liquid that is attractive to inquisitive puppies. It is also very toxic.

If you think your puppy may have been in contact with something that might be dangerous, don't delay. Call your vet and take your puppy straight round there. If you have a container with details of any chemicals, etc., take this with you as it could give your vet vital, life-saving clues as to which treatment is needed.

AND FINALLY ...

Your family and your puppy can look forward to many years of happy times together. You have already shown that you are a responsible and caring owner by buying this booklet. We hope we have given you 'paws for thought' (sorry!) and that the advice we have given is useful.

If we had to give just a few words of advice to a new puppy owner, they would be:

Insure your puppy
Take him to a well-run puppy class
Keep his social calendar as full as possible
Enjoy him!

All puppies can be trained to a high level and the time and effort taken will be amply rewarded in the years ahead. Work hard now, then sit back and reap the rewards of owning a well-behaved, well socialised dog who is a joy to you and a constant source of pride.

HAVE FUN!

I HAVE SOCIALISED MY PUPPY WITH ...

Your puppy needs to have had GOOD experiences of everything listed below while he is under 20 weeks old. Be sensible, be calm, be inventive.

NEVER force your dog into a situation he isn't comfortable with. If he's unsure, then casually let him make up his own mind from a distance and then praise him when he shows interest. Don't reassure, as he might think he's being praised for his fear. Simply let him take his own sweet time about it.

PEOPLE

- Adult men & women of various ethnic groups ❑
- Children aged 0 - 6 months ❑
- Toddlers ❑
- Children aged 6 years ❑
- Children aged 12 years ❑
- Children in pushchairs ❑
- Person with walking stick ❑
- Man with a beard ❑
- Person wearing a hat ❑
- Person wearing sunglasses ❑
- Person wearing a uniform ❑
- Person who delivers the post/milk/newspapers ❑
- Strangers outside the house ❑
- Strangers coming into the house ❑
- People on bicycles & rollerskates ❑

DOGS ...

- Other puppies at the vets ❑
- Other puppies at socialisation class ❑
- Black dogs ❑
- Dogs with short muzzles (e.g. Bulldog, Boxer) ❑
- Dogs with heavy coats (e.g. Old English Sheepdog) ❑
- Small dogs (e.g., Jack Russell Terrier, Shih Tzu) ❑
- Big dogs ❑
- Dogs held in someone's arms ❑

ENVIRONMENTS ...

- Busy town centre ❑
- Walking past school playground at play time ❑
- Railway Stations ❑
- The Vets Waiting Room ❑
- The Countryside ❑
- The car ❑
- Other people's cars ❑
- Other people's homes ❑
- Other people's gardens ❑
- Grooming Parlour ❑
- City Farm ❑
- Parks ❑
- Seaside ❑
- Sand dunes ❑

OBJECTS ...

- Bin bags caught on railings/in tree ❑
- Balloons ❑
- Aeroplanes ❑
- Helicopters ❑
- Shopping Trolleys ❑
- Christmas Trees ❑
- Halloween Masks ❑
- Motorised Children's Toys ❑
- Other animals e.g. ❑
  - cats ❑
  - rabbits ❑
  - guinea pigs ❑
  - livestock (sheep, cattle, etc.) ❑

This list is by no means exhaustive so use your imagination. Introduce your puppy to the rich pageant of human life.